SMOKED
COCKTAILS

. . . .

FROM MIXOLOGY TO SMOKING
TECHNIQUES

Benji O'Day

Contents

BASICS

The official definition of "cocktail", according to the Merriam-Webster Dictionary, is "a chilled beverage of distilled wine or liquor mixed with flavouring ingredients". While this is a rather broad definition, it reflects the modern practice of referring to almost any mixed beverage as a cocktail.

The first published definition of a cocktail appeared in an editorial response in The Balance and Columbian Repository in 1806. It read: 'Cocktail is a stimulating liquor, consisting of spirits of any kind, sugar, water and bitters'. This is the accepted definition of the ingredients used today when talking about the 'ideal' cocktail.

A (Brief) History

They might look right at the top of a glass, but a small paper umbrella and an orange peel do not make a cocktail. Nor does fruit juice or soda when added to a shot of rum or vodka (if we're being really technical, these aren't 'cocktails' at all). So what exactly does a cocktail do? A few things, mainly alcohol, water, sugar and bitters. But also a lot of history.

Cocktails are traditionally considered an American innovation, but in fact they were at least partly inspired by British punches: large bowls of spirits mixed with fruit juice, spices and other flavours, consumed in punch houses in the 18th century. The term cocktail was even first seen in a British newspaper printed in March 1798. But the term was not really defined as we know it until 1806, when The Balance and Columbian Repository of Hudson, New York, attributed the cocktail to what we follow today: 'a stimulating liquor composed of any kind of sugar, water and bitters, vulgarly called a bitter slingshot'. (The slingshot actually preceded the cocktail, basically the same thing made without bitters).

"Stimulating" has always been a fundamental primary objective of cocktails, but the true art of the bartender evolved thanks largely to one guy, Jerry Thomas. Jerry, aka "Professor" Thomas, a prolific Connecticut-born

American bartender who worked all over America and Europe and wrote one of the first comprehensive recipe books - The Bartender's Guide (or How to Mix Drinks), basically an encyclopaedia of mixed drinks that has become a standard bearer for bartenders.

Not that Thomas and his colleagues were working in a vacuum. Increased travel and moves towards industrialisation helped, as did innovations towards a key ingredient in cocktail culture: ice. Imagine going to a bar and getting everything from a Mint Julep to a room temperature Martini. We don't have to, thanks to a guy crazy enough to dream up an ice export business at a time when the fastest delivery system was a ship and most ports weren't equipped to store ice that didn't melt in transit. This did not deter Frederic "Ice King" Tudor, who kept trying and failing to transport ice from colder climates to warmer ports until the venture finally succeeded (and made him a billionaire). With ice more readily available around the US and internationally, the possibilities for cocktails and drinks exploded.

But then a little thing called Prohibition put a slight damper on cocktail consumption (and gave a big boost to organised crime). Even after its repeal, many of our most talented bartenders had already found new homes abroad. In a way, the World Wars (and increased tourism) were a slight saving grace for cocktail culture, with exposure to the Pacific theatre and its Polynesian culture introducing us to the kitsch and rum galore of what has become our corrupt tiki culture. Ernest Raymond Beaumont Gantt's adopted character, Don the Beachcomber, became a Hollywood icon and Polynesian hot spot, while Victor Bergereon (aka "Trader Vic") opened a self-named competing Tiki spot in San Francisco in the 1930s.

The focus on the Tiki gave way to a focus on other cocktail cultures, and by the mid-20th century, cocktail culture was on a slight upswing - think Mad Men, Manhattans, Martini lunches - just to take a step back while the drug cultures of the 1960s and 1970s strutted forward. It wasn't until the 1990s or so that a modest but ambitious group of bartenders led by the likes of Dale Degroff at New York's famed Rainbow Room began to revive the classic cocktail culture of the Thomas era, bringing back historical values and rigid standards of quality to a craft that had morphed into sour mixes, pre-made bottled cocktails like The Pink Squirrel, and shooters like Training Bra. (The decades that followed Degroff saw what became a renaissance of 'mixology').

Classic and even historic cocktails might be more readily available, but many of the drinks found in The Bartender's Guide probably won't make it to the bar menu any time soon, which is a shame, because they have fun names like Brandy Crusta and Port Wine Sangaree. So while you can't order a Duke of Norfolk Punch (brandy, wine, milk and sugar) in most bars, you can get a decent Milk Punch or even (if you're really lucky) watch a really skilled bartender pour liquid fire for Professor Thomas's Blue Blazer. (Because liquid fire never goes out of style).

The First Cocktails

People have been mixing drinks for centuries, often to make an ingredient more palatable or to create medicinal elixirs. It wasn't until the 17th and 18th centuries that cocktail precursors (e.g. slings, fizzes, toddies and juleps) became popular enough to be recorded in history books. Although it is unclear where, who, and what went into creating the original cocktail, it began as a specific drink formula rather than a category of mixed drinks.

The first published reference to the cocktail appears in the Farmer's Cabinet (Amherst, New Hampshire, 28 April 1803). The editorial parody tells of a 'cot' who, with an 11am hangover, '...drank a glass of cocktail - good for the head...'. In his book "Imbibe!", David Wondrich attributes the first known recipe for the printed cocktail to Captain J.E. Alexander in 1831. It called for brandy, gin or rum in a mixture of "...one third spirit to two thirds water; add bitters, and enrich with sugar and nutmeg...".

The formula of the original 'cocktail' recipe lives on. The brandy cocktail, for example, is a mix of brandy, orange curaçao (the sweetener) and bitters, shaken with ice (the water). Since it is most often served with a lemon twist, it is technically a 'fancy brandy cocktail'. By replacing the base spirit, other classics such as gin, rum or whisky cocktails are created.

Origins Of The Name

For 15 years I have been trying to understand why we call a cocktail a cocktail and where this useful little invention came from. Not long ago, my search saw me poking around a quiet old churchyard in the pleasant town of Lewiston, New York, where Catherine Hustler, the woman who surely invented the cocktail, sleeps. More recently, he found me fiddling with my phone in London's busy Borough High Street, just south of London Bridge, as the lunchtime crowd swirled around me, trying to get a decent picture of an anodyne modern office building distinguished only by the three sculpted blue musicians walking, for reasons of their own, straight up its facade. Here, 300 years before the arrival of the blue musicians, was the pharmacy of one Richard Stoughton, who probably also invented the cocktail.

The history of the cocktail - and here I mean the original cocktail, the mixture of spirits, bitters, sugar and water that spawned the whole seductive tribe - has always (perhaps unsurprisingly) been like this: heady with red herrings and punctuated by treacherous maybes. Indeed, while it has become much easier to find an actual cocktail in the last 15 years, the state of knowledge about the cocktail's origin and etymology has not progressed much since William Grimes summed it up in his 1991 landmark history of American mixology, Straight Up or On the Rocks: "The word 'cocktail' ... remains one of the most elusive in the language."

There are many stories behind the origin of the name "cocktail". As always, some are just myths or folklore, others are credible, and more than a few may have probably been exaggerated over the years by inebriated or imaginative bartenders. One may even be the truth. Nevertheless, the stories are fascinating.

One famous story behind the cocktail's name refers to the tail of a rooster (or rooster's tail), which served as a garnish for a colonial drink. In written recipes there are no formal references to such a garnish.

- In James Fenimore Cooper's 1821 novel, The Spy, the character "Betty Flanagan" invented the cocktail during the Revolution. "Betty" may have referred to an actual innkeeper at Four Corners in upstate New York City by the name of Catherine "Kitty" Hustler. Betty assumed another essayist's face, that of Betsy Flanagan. Betsy probably wasn't a real woman, but the story goes that she was an innkeeper who served French soldiers a drink in 1779 garnished with the tail feathers of a neighbour's rooster. Within this complicated mix of stories, it is generally assumed that Kitty inspired Betty and Betty inspired Betsy.

- It is also said that the rooster theory was influenced by the colours of the mixed ingredients, which can resemble the colours of the rooster's tail. Considering the colourful array of ingredients used in the modern bar, this might be a good story today. At the time, however, the drinks were visually bland.

- In 1936, the British publication Bartender published a ten-year history of British sailors being served mixed drinks in Mexico. A cola de gallo (rooster's tail) - a long plant root shaped like a bird's tail - was used to mix the drinks.

- One cocktail story refers to the leftovers from a beer barrel, called cock tailings. Cock tailings of various spirits were mixed and sold as a cheap mixed drink of (understandably) questionable integrity.

- Another unappetising origin tells of a cock ale, a beer mash mixed with whatever was available to feed fighting cocks.

- "'Cocktail' may derive from the French term for a cup of eggs, coquetel. One story that brought this reference to America speaks of Antoine Amedie Peychaud of New Orleans, who mixed his Peychaud Bitters into a stomach remedy served in a coquetel. Not all of Peychaud's customers could pronounce the word, and it became known as a cocktail. Due to conflicting dates, however, this story does not add up.

- The word cocktail may be a distant derivation of the name of the Aztec goddess, Xochitl (SHO-cheetl, meaning 'flower' in Nahuatl). Xochitl was also the name of a Mexican princess who served drinks to American soldiers.

- It was an 18th- and 19th-century custom to dock the tails of draft horses, which caused the tail to rise like a rooster's tail. According to the story, a reader's letter to The Balance and Columbian Repository explains that, when drunk, these cocktails made your tail "stand up" in the same way.

- Another horse story supposes the influence of a breeder's term for a mixed-breed horse, or cock-tail. Both racing and drinking were popular among most Americans at the time; the name may have passed from mixed breeds to mixed drinks.

- There is a bizarre story of an American innkeeper who stored alcohol in a ceramic container shaped like a rooster. When patrons wanted another round, they touched the rooster's tail.

- There is a bizarre story of an American innkeeper who stored alcohol in a ceramic container in the shape of a rooster. When patrons wanted another round, they touched the rooster's tail.

- In George Bishop's 1965 book, 'The Booze Reader: A Soggy Saga of Man in His Cups', he writes: 'The word itself derives from the English rooster's tail which, in the mid-nineteenth century, referred to a woman of easy virtue, desirable but impure... and applied to the new American habit of "contaminating" good British Gin with foreign matter, including ice'. Yes, ice was once a controversial topic in the bar!

The Storyline

500-1800
The cock's tail

Mixed drinks have existed since the 1500s - mulled wine, posset pouch and toddy were consumed then. But the term "cocktail" was not coined until later. There are many stories about its origins. There is talk of a beautiful girl named Coctel who served the king of Mexico and an American general at the signing of a peace treaty in 1800. The invention of the word is attributed to Frenchman Antoine AmédéePeychaud, the creator of Peychaud's Bitters, who served a concoction of bitters and brandy as a remedy for an upset stomach in an egg cup, called coquetier in French.

The most popular story is about the French soldiers who helped the Americans fight for independence in 1770. A barmaid named Betsy Flanagan served them drinks decorated with colourful feathers from a rooster's tail.

One of the first recorded appearances of the word cocktail in print was in a New York newspaper called the Balance & Columbian Repository, on 13 May 1806. A cocktail was described as "a stimulating liquor, consisting of spirits of any kind, sugar, water and bitters - it is vulgarly called a bittered sling". Drinking historians and authors Jared Brown and Anistatia

Miller found the word in a 1798 edition of a London newspaper called the Morning Post & Gazetteer. It appears in reference to a politician's debt in a pub near Downing Street.

1800-1900
America's Golden Age

At the beginning of the 19th century, sazerac (rye whisky or cognac with absinthe and bitters) and brandy crustaceans (cognac, Grand Marnier and Maraschino) were born in New Orleans. In the 1850s, whisky sours appeared. Then, the first bottles of vermouth landed on American shores and a cocktail of rye whisky and vermouth called Manhattan appeared. Bartender and author of The Joy of Mixology, Gary Regan says the Manhattan was the first cocktail to use vermouth. "From it came the martinez and the martini."

The first American cocktails used mainly cognac, rum or American whisky. The only white spirit used was gin. Vodka, now the basis of many popular cocktails, was not yet in the picture. In 1862, the first ever book on bartending was published, The Bartender's Guide by Jerry Thomas. Thomas, popularly known as The Professor, is often called the godfather of the American bartending industry. His book contained some of the earliest recipes for homemade bar syrups, bottled cocktails and jello shots. In 1882, Harry 'The Dean' Johnson, another important figure in the history of the American bartender, published the Bartender's Manual. It contained the oldest known reference to the classic gin martini, stirred, not shaken.

The 19th century was a golden age for cocktails in the United States. Bartending was among the highest paying professions. Thomas was one of the most influential people in San Francisco and reportedly earned more than the Vice President. Remember that back then bartenders didn't have access to syrups or ready-made purees; everything was made from scratch. The drinks they created are still drunk today.

Even the ice used in a cocktail got a lot of attention back then. In their two-part encyclopaedic discourse on spirits and cocktails, Spirituous Journey: A History of Drinking, Brown and Miller tell us that in the 1830s, blocks of ice were being harvested from frozen lakes in Boston and shipped to the southern states of America and Cuba. This ice would make its way to Calcutta, where the British used it to chill their wines and beers. Tell your local bartender that next time he will be stingy with the ice.

1900-1933
Crossing the Atlantic

The cocktail industry lost momentum when the Temperance Movement swept through the United States in the early 1900s. It led to prohibition in the

United States, which outlawed the sale, consumption, production and transportation of alcohol in the United States, and lasted from 1920 to 1933. Smuggled alcohol became popular, and many distillers left the big cities to distill in the forests or in Canada and then smuggle the alcohol into the United States. This gave rise to a phenomenon called 'rum running', which referred to smugglers trying to evade excise officials. Many of the first American NASCAR racers were rum runners during Prohibition.

America's famous bars were replaced by illegal ones, called speakeasies. While some bartenders found other careers, others emigrated to Europe and found work in bars in big cities like London and Paris. Very soon, American drinkers who could not do without their old fashioned and martinis sought out these bars. Thus, London and Paris had their first 'American bars'. Bars in opulent hotels, such as the Savoy, in London, or the Ritz, in Paris, became a mecca for cocktails.

1933-1990
Vodka conquers the world

Prohibition ended in 1933, but World War II meant that times remained tumultuous for the US liquor industry. Only after that did vodka enter America. It had its work cut out for it in a country that guzzled copious amounts of beer, whisky and rum. At the time, rum-based Polynesian Tiki cocktails, such as mai tais and planter's punch, were all the rage in North America.

In the 1950s, some young Americans began drinking vodka mixed with ginger ale, a drink called the Moscow Mule. Then, in 1962, a certain British spy announced to filmgoers on both sides of the Atlantic that he liked his martinis with vodka, shaken, not stirred, and vodka was the new favourite ingredient in cocktails. In the last two decades more cocktails have been made with vodka than any other spirit.

1990-2000
Quantity over quality

The emergence of bar chains such as Thank God it's Friday in the early 1990s corrupted the cocktail to some extent. Instead of finely crafted drinks served in elegant glassware, they were quickly put together in crude jugs. Customers got good value for money, but the art of mixing drinks was almost lost.

2000-2013
The renaissance

The last 13 years or so have seen the emergence of modern classics, such as the breakfast martini (a gin martini with jam), invented by Salvatore Calabrese at

London's Library Bar, and the emergence of craft bars, such as New York's Milk & Honey.

Matthew Pomeroy, the global brand ambassador for Absolut Vodka, says the past 10 years have seen a resurgence in craft drinks. "A new focus on fruit juices and fresh herbs has taken the bartender's art to a new level," he says, "while the internet and reprints of old cocktail books allow modern bartenders to read and research old classics."

Cocktails have come a long way since they were first mixed. They've helped the food and drink industry grow, they've created jobs and, most importantly, they've helped people bond. Now, if you'll excuse me, I'm going to go sip my old fashioned while I read The Deans of Drinks, a book about two bartenders from the early 1900s, Harry Johnson and Harry Craddock.

Mixology: A Definition

Mixology', or 'mixologist', is defined as 'the art or skill of preparing mixed drinks'. The originality of this method of cocktail preparation is based on combining substances of different natures and consistencies, balancing the flavours of the ingredients with balance and originality. Thanks to special mixing techniques, it is possible to skilfully combine different elements such as plant extracts and spices with wines and spirits. Today this word has become quite common to indicate the bartender who uses his knowledge of preparation and study of spirits and distillates to create innovative drinks, with increasingly sophisticated techniques for the most refined palates.

The discipline was invented by Jerry Thomas, a bartender who sailed for California during the gold rush period in the mid-19th century. Regarded by the New York Times as the forerunner of bartending, he wrote The Bar-Tender's Guide in 1862, in which he meticulously explained the oldest oral recipes and his own creations of "mixed drinks".

Mixology, also known as Molecular and Physical Gastronomy, was then developed around the 1980s thanks to the studies of Nicholas Kurti, a Hungarian physicist, and Hervé This, a French chemist. The creation of a good cocktail, according to this theory, requires the bartender to follow a scientific approach in the mixing of flavours and colours, of different densities and consistencies among the various gastronomic products. In the 1990s it spread to the English-speaking world and became one of the most popular techniques in lounge bars.

Because mixology means "mixing logic", i.e. combining various ingredients in order to mix them in a balanced way, bartenders who follow this discipline must be trained not only in the science of cooking, but also in the history of cocktails and master various preparation techniques.

In fact, mixology offers reinterpretations of traditional alcoholic beverages: from liqueurs to spices, jellies to fresh fruits, it is therefore important to know all the ingredients well in order to create or reinvent something original. But the real strength is the enhancement of the customer's experience: with elegant movements, a compact style and a refined and fascinating explanation of the drink, the bartender captivates the customer to enhance the drinking experience.

COKTAILS 101

How many times have you heard your favourite cocktail associated with terms you didn't know existed? It happens to everyone, especially if you are not a mixology expert. But it's not at all difficult to remedy this shortcoming. In this post, you'll find out what categories cocktails fall into, the large families into which they are divided. You should know that drinks are classified by function, quantity and family.

The division by function includes:

- pre dinner or aperitifs
- after dinner and all time cocktails
- long drinks or thirst quenchers

While the classification by quantity is as follows:

- short drinks: between 6 and 9 cl
- medium drink: between 10 and 12 cl
- long drink: over 12 cl

Now that we've learned the basics, here's the third type of classification, by family. Below you will find the most common cocktail categories and their characteristics.

Cocktail Families

COBBLER

This family includes medium and long thirst-quenching drinks which are characterised by the presence of pieces of fresh fruit and crushed ice. The cocktail is then completed with a good dose of spirits, liqueur or sparkling wine and in some cases fruit or sugar syrup. These drinks are served with straws and a spoon.

The most famous examples? Bramble and Sherry Cobbler.

DAISY

This group includes medium drinks and all-day cocktails in which lemon juice and grenadine or horchata syrup are added to the alcohol base, which is often brandy. This type of cocktail is prepared by shaking the ingredients in a shaker and served in a tumbler glass filled with ice, diluted with soda. A famous example is the Brandy Daisy.

FIZZ

The term fizz is used to describe a series of thirst-quenching long drinks consisting of distillate, lime (or lemon) juice, sugar syrup and soda. The ingredients are shaken in the shaker and the cocktail is served in a tumbler glass with ice. The most famous example is of course the Gin Fizz.

FROZEN

This category includes thirst-quenching medium and long drinks that are made in a blender and consist of spirits, fruit, citrus juices, aromatic liqueurs, syrups, sugar and lots of ice. At the end the cocktail will have a very pleasant consistency, similar to that of a light slush. One of the most famous cocktails is the Frozen

Daiquiri. But Mai Tais and Margaritas in the frozen version are also famous.

GROG

A family of hot short drinks that are prepared with a distillate or liqueur diluted in boiling water, enriched with spices, citrus peels and sugar. Sometimes a curl of butto is also added! These drinks are served in small glasses with a handle. The family takes its name from the most famous of these drinks, the Grog.

JULEP

This group includes the "relatives" of the Mojito. This kind of cocktail is very similar, the big difference being that the ingredients are shaken in the shaker. Among these drinks the Mint Julep is the best known.

POUNDED

One of the most famous families of drinks. The must-have ingredients for these cocktails are chopped lime and sugar. They originate in the Caribbean and have a low alcohol content, making them thirst-quenching and suitable for high temperatures. The most famous are the Mojito, Caipirinha and Caipiroska.

RICKEYS

Similar to crushed drinks, these drinks are prepared in the glass with ice cubes and a light distillate made from crushed lime (or lemon) and sugar. Compared to pestates, however, they are less sweet, made with gin and diluted with soda. As the name suggests, the most famous is the Gin Rickey.

SHRUB-CUP

A family of pre-dinner and thirst-quenching long drinks which includes cocktails prepared in large quantities and served in large jugs. They are made with a base of distillate and fresh fruit, sugar, lemon and spices. Sangria is certainly the best known example.

SOUR

This category includes medium aperitif drinks and all time cocktails made with distillate, lemon juice and sugar syrup. Their characteristic is that they have a taste that is neither sweet nor sour. They are served filtered or with ice in a goblet glass. The most popular are Whiskey Sour, White lady, Daiquiri, Margarita and Pisco sour.

SPARKILING
This family includes all those medium and long thirst-quenching drinks that are perfect for the aperitif because they are prepared by combining fruit pulp or nectar and sparkling wine. Light and refined cocktails,

related to the Spritz. Among the most famous are the Bellini and the Kir Royal.

Formulas: The Great Disagreement

Maybe you don't realise that there are a lot of disagreements in bartending. I mean, sure, people argue all the time while drinking. But those fights are usually about complex topics like religion, politics and sports rivalries. Disagreements about bartending? What is there to disagree about?

One source of disagreement is proportions and formulas for specific drinks. I like to think of it in terms of proportions-1 part X: 2 parts Y: 3 parts Z, for example. David Embury, writer of the 1948 classic The Fine Art of Mixing Drinks, discusses the wide range of proportions found when studying recipes: 'As with other drinks, proportions vary all over the map, according to the personal whims and individual taste of the recipe's author'.

He cites one recipe calling for 1 part sweet, 2 parts acid, 3 parts strong (with "strong" meaning the base spirit), and another calling for 6 parts acid to 1 part strong. What Embury saw in 1948 still stands today. Some swear by the recipe 1 part sweet, 2 acid, 3 strong; others like a recipe 1 part sweet, 2 acid, 4 strong.

Embury's advice? One part sweet, 2 parts sour, 8 parts strong.

Now, I've tried that recipe. Basically, for a single cocktail, that translates to 2 ounces of spirit, 1/2 ounce of citrus juice, 1/4 ounce of simple syrup or liqueur. The first problem I have with that recipe is that it's a small cocktail. Second, it's too dry for my taste, and it's a little too alcoholic.

In the aforementioned Joy of Mixology, Gary Regan also discusses the controversy over proportions. He discusses Embury's approach and comes to a similar conclusion: it is too acidic. Regan proposes the following proportion for making a Sidecar: 3 parts strong, 2 parts sweet and 1 part acid. Yes, you read that right; it is a sour in which the sweetness is higher than the sour.

It can be debated whether this is the right way to make such a drink, but guess what? Regan would agree with you; he presents his preference and then concludes: 'The cocktailian bartender should experiment for himself'.

Disagreement even spilled over into the comments section of last week's post. (Disagreement in a comments section? I'm shocked-SHOCKED!-to hear about it). Someone linked to a recipe by David Wondrich for a Whiskey Sour. Wondrich's interpretation of this drink calls for 2 ounces of bourbon, 2/3 of lemon juice, and 1 teaspoon of sugar.

This is... even more acidic than Embury's formula, which calls for 1/2 ounce of citrus.

But bourbon is bourbon, and it's sweet on its own, so I can see it working. I don't think it would work with rye whiskey, though, and I'm not sure of its merits with a dry, well-aged cognac.

My point is this: You can't take a single formula or recipe and apply it to every cocktail you can make. A specific Manhattan recipe that works great with Rittenhouse Rye and Dolin Rouge vermouth might taste terrible with Maker's Mark and Cinzano.

Regan suggests tasting all your ingredients yourself before you start mixing, and that's great advice. Know the flavour profile of each ingredient and then start thinking about how well it will mix with the others.

Speaking for myself, I don't have a standard formula that I use for, say, all types of ingredients. With a Sidecar, my palate finds balance in a recipe that almost equals sweet and sour. With a Daiquiri, on the other hand, I like them dry and sour. A teaspoon of sugar and 3/4 ounce of lime: perfect.

Mixology Glossary

- Box: Pour in and out of a shaker, usually only once. Gives the drink a quick stir without shaking.

- Call Drink: A liqueur and a mixer, of which the liqueur is a defined brand. (e.g. Tanqueray and Tonic, Bacardi and Coca Cola)

- Cobbler: A tall drink of any liquor served in a collins or highball glass with crushed or shaved ice and garnished with fresh fruit and sprigs of mint.

- Chaser: A mixer that is consumed immediately after a shot of liquor to create a different flavour.

- Cocktail: Any of a variety of alcoholic drinks usually consisting of brandy, whisky, vodka or gin combined with fruit juices or other liqueurs and often served cold.

- Collins: A sour-like drink that is served in a tall glass with soda water or seltzer water.

- Cooler: A drink consisting of ginger ale, sparkling water and a fresh spiral or twist of citrus peel, served in a collins or highball glass.

- Crust: A sour drink served in a glass completely lined with orange or lemon peel cut into continuous strips.

- Cup: A punch-type drink that was made up in quantities of cups or glasses in preference to a punch bowl.

- Daisy: A large sour-type drink, usually made with rum or gin. It is served over crushed ice with a straw and sweetened with fruit syrup.

- Lace: Normally applied to the last ingredient in a recipe, i.e. poured over the top of the drink.

- Zabaione: A traditional holiday drink containing a combination of beaten eggs with cream or milk, sugar and a liqueur such as brandy, rum or bourbon.

- Fix: A sour type drink similar to daisy, made with crushed ice in a large glass.

- Fizz: An effervescent drink. (i.e. one that is carbonated or emits small bubbles).

- Flip: A cold, creamy drink made from eggs, sugar and wine or liqueur. Brandy and sherry flips are two of the most popular types.

- Frappé: A partially frozen, often fruity drink. It is usually a mixture of ingredients served on a pile of crushed ice.

- Grog: A drink made from rum with water, fruit juice and sugar, commonly served in a large mug.

- Highball: Any spirit served with ice and soda in a medium to tall glass (often a highball glass).

- Julep: A drink made from bourbon, mint, sugar and crushed ice.

- Lowball: A short alcohol-based drink served with ice, water or soda in a small glass.

- Mist: A liquor served over a glass filled with crushed ice, often a way of serving liquor as an after-dinner drink.

- Mulls: A warmed sweetened and spiced liquor, wine or beer, served as a hot punch.

- Smooth: The consumption of a spirit as a straight shot, unaccompanied.

- Negus: A punch-like combination containing a wine, such as port, heated with spices and sweetened.

- Nip: A quarter bottle.

- Nightcap: A wine or liquor taken before going to bed.

- On the rocks: A wine or liquor poured over ice cubes.

- Pick-Me-Up: A drink designed to alleviate the effects of overindulgence in alcohol.

- Posset: An old British drink from which eggnog was made. It consists of a mixture of warm beer or wine curdled with milk, eggs and spices.

- Puff: A traditional afternoon drink made from equal parts alcohol and milk, topped with club soda and served over ice.

- Punch: A party drink consisting of fruit, fruit juices, flavours and sweeteners, soft drinks and a wine or liquor base.

- Rickey: A drink made from a liqueur, usually gin, half a lime and sparkling water. It is sometimes sweetened, and often served with ice in a rickey glass.

- Sangaree: A tall, cold, sweetened wine/liqueur garnished with nutmeg.

- Shooter: A shot of whisky or other spirit taken neat.

- Shrub: Liqueurs, fruit juices and sugar, aged in a sealed container such as a cask or crock, then usually bottled.

- Slingshot: A tall drink made from brandy, whisky or gin, with lemon juice, sugar and sparkling water. It is served both hot and cold.

- Smash: A short julep of liquor, sugar and mint, served in a shot glass.

- Sour: A short drink consisting of liqueur, lemon/lime juice and sugar.

- Supercall: Also known as top shelf or super premium. High octane versions, often higher alcohol proof, or super-aged or flavoured.

- Swizzle: A tall cocktail, traditionally rum-based, filled with cracked ice. A stirring rod or stick is quickly swirled between the palms of the hands to form the ice on the glass.

- Syllabub: A drink made from a mixture of sweetened milk/cream, wine and spices.

- Toddy: A sweetened drink of liquor and hot water, often with spices and served in a tall glass.

- Tot: A small amount of liquor.

- Virgin: A non-alcoholic drink.

- Drink well: A liqueur and a mixer, the brands of which are not defined. (i.e. Gin and Tonic, Rum and Coca-Cola)

25 Classic Cocktails You Should Know

Those of us who like to mix drinks at home do so for many reasons: First, it's cheaper than drinking out. Second, it's fun to mix your own drinks at home. Third, it is even more fun to mix drinks for others at home. Any self-respecting bartender at home should have a mental Excel spreadsheet with favourite classic cocktail recipes. Even if these aren't fully memorised, you should be able to find the recipe in your home library at a moment's notice to serve to your friends.

Today I present to you the 25 essential drinks that I think everyone should be able to make. I'm not including any highballs. If you can't mix a gin and tonic or a whiskey and soda without a recipe, you might want to do some catch-up reading (and drinking!) first. But if you get to the end of this list and are thirsty for more, we've got you covered.

The Old Fashioned
The origins of the word 'cocktail' are lost in history, but the first definition we find in print comes from an 1806 New York State newspaper. A cocktail is called "a stimulating liquor, consisting of spirits of any kind, sugar, water and bitters...". Over the course of the

19th century, the cocktail underwent a series of additions and refinements: liqueurs, fortified wines, various pieces of garnish, etc. Eventually, some drinkers came to prefer a simpler form of cocktail, the kind that might have appealed to their grandparents, and so they asked the bartender to make them an "old-fashioned" cocktail of spirits, sugar mixed with water to form a syrup, and bitters. If you want to try the ur-cocktail, or if you just want to enjoy some treats, the Old Fashioned is the drink for you.

Note that the original definition called for alcohol of any kind. You can make a tasty Old Fashioned from whisky, of course, but also from tequila, mezcal, brandy, rum, genever and, to a lesser extent, aquavit or gin. I've also been desperate enough to try an old fashioned vodka, but I can't say I've enjoyed it. Stick with liquors with a more robust flavour.

Martinez

The grandfather of the modern martini, the Martinez is a drink made with gin (Old Tom, if possible; try Ransom or Hayman's), sweet vermouth, maraschino or curaçao, and bitters. It is a sweeter drink than the typical dry martini, but the flavour is complex and refreshing. Assembling the ingredients requires some outlay of funds, but if you're within walking distance of a reputable craft cocktail bar, you should be able to sample one.

I wouldn't say that a Martinez is on my weekly cocktail list, but I do sample one every few months or so. I consider the drink important not only from a historical point of view, but also as a taste of how diverse the cocktail world can be.

Martini

And here's the grandson, though now venerable in his own right. Within reason, this one can be mixed however you like, and it's still a martini. Make it extra wet with equal parts gin and vermouth. Make it ultradry with a simple dollop of vermouth. Shake. Stir. Garnish with an olive, a lemonade, an onion, a slice of cucumber.

Manhattan

If there were no other reason to include this drink on this list, I would still put the Manhattan here for the best reason of all: your grandmother drinks them.

Now, I'm pretty flexible on the Old Fashioned and Martini. Mix an OF with mezcal or agricultural rum and I'll shake your hand; shake an ultra-dry martini and I'll happily drink it. But please, no weak bourbon in my Manhattan. Give me a bourbon with a muscular rye mashbill, or give me some rye for that matter. Mix it sweet or mix it perfectly (half sweet vermouth, half dry), but don't bother with a dry Manhattan, seriously.

Brooklyn

A Manhattan variant that launched a cocktail family of its own. The Brooklyn adapts the formula for a perfect Manhattan, which is rye or bourbon, dry vermouth and sweet vermouth. The Brooklyn swaps the sweet for a mixture of maraschino liqueur and bitters. Historically, it has required Amer Picon, which is very difficult to find in the United States. Ramazotti can be used instead of Picon.

In fact, you can use many things in place of Picon. If you use Punt e Mes, you have a Red Hook cocktail, named after the Brooklyn borough. Other Brooklyn nabes lend their name to other Brooklyn variations. The Greenpoint uses Chartreuse (yellow, though, oddly enough); the Bensonhurst calls for Cynar; and the Bushwick calls for Carpano Antica vermouth in addition to Amer Picon and maraschino. My current Brooklyn hangouts are Kensington and Ditmas Park, and a quick search turned up no Brooklyn variants named after those neighborhoods. I'd have to work on that.

Daiquiri

Here, with the daiquiri, you have what I call a perfect litmus cocktail. Whenever I pick up a new rum, I almost always want to try it two different ways: on the rocks and mixed into a daiquiri. I find that the lime and sugar in a daiquiri complement the rum and enhance the flavours. I learn more about a rum mixed in a daiquiri than I do sipping it on its own. The only exception, I find, are rich and funky rums, such as agricultural rums. These tend to overpower the other ingredients.

Margarita

I'd like to say that everyone remembers their first Margarita, but we all know that's not true. I think it's also possible that no one remembers their first Margarita.

I admit, sometimes when I'm out to dinner at a Mexican or Tex-Mex place and I want a Margarita, I don't always care if it's made with fresh or pre-mixed ingredients. But I will never buy premix for my home bar, and neither should you. The margarita is a simple recipe, just three ingredients, so there's no excuse for premix. Get a good tequila (100% agave), a decent triple sec, and fresh lime, and you're almost guaranteed a great drink.

Sidecar

An unlikely cousin to the Margarita, the Sidecar falls into the same Sour family as the tequila classic. In fact, once you know how to make a Margarita from memory, you pretty much know how to make a Sidecar: they're pretty much the same drink. One uses tequila and lime, while the other calls for cognac and lemon, but the pattern is witty, orange liqueur and citrus.

What always amazes me, though, is how the character of the base spirit changes the feel of the drink. A Margarita feels like summer to me, drinking outside on a bright, hot day. A Sidecar, on the other hand, because of the warmth and smoothness of the cognac, feels like a drink to be sipped, if not by the fire, then certainly in a dark bar on a cool autumn night. These drinks may have a common pedigree, but they are as individual as feuding sisters.

French 75

If you're a cocktail geek, and you don't have the French 75 in your party repertoire, sorry, but you're not a cocktail geek. I brought the makings of the French 75 to some new friends' houses a few years ago, and although my wife and I started the evening as the only gin fans in the house, I ended up converting everyone else to the cause that night. You can't count on much in life, but you can always expect sparkling cocktails to sound good at parties.

Bloody Mary

I'm breaking my highball rule, but that's okay because I don't think of the Bloody Mary as a highball. Although almost every cocktail manual I own lists it as such, I see it differently. A highball simply means pouring a shot of alcohol and filling it with a non-alcoholic mixer, usually from a gun or bottle. Well, you can make Bloody Marys this way if you're lazy and buy a mix in a bottle. But a good Bloody Mary mix is made at home with high quality tomato juice and any other juice and spices you like. To drink at home, I mix my own à la minute. I juice the lemons; I dip into the bitters. I go to work at least as much as I work when I mix a cocktail. So screw it, it's a cocktail, not a highball.

Irish Coffee

Unfortunately, we may have strayed from the breakfast/brunch cocktail. If someone tells you that Irish Coffee is a sweet drink, scald it with your coffee. Just a little sugar, your Irish, your coffee and a dollop of lightly whipped cream on top.

Jack Rose

A deceptively simple looking recipe, the Jack Rose involves the use of apple juice, lime juice and grenadine. The way these flavours blend together is simply delicious. Make your own grenadine - it's quick and easy. (Although bottled pomegranate juice will do; you don't need to make your own juice). Take the time and spend the money to track down Laird's Bonded Apple Brandy for this one, too. It has a rich, fresh apple flavour that is much more satisfying than even Laird's blended applejack sells. (The blended product mixes apple brandy with neutral grain brandy. It's tastier than an apple vodka, but nowhere near as tasty as the blended).

Negroni

I don't think I understand people who don't like Negronis. The blend of bitter and sweet, the complexity of the herbs, the refreshing pleasure - you'd have to be crazy not to love this. Like the Martini, the Negroni is a drink open to manipulation. You start with the classic 1:1:1 ratio and go from there. It's fun. Also try mixing vermouths. Right now I like a Negroni that is 2 parts gin, 1 part Campari and 1/2 part Carpano Antica and Martini & Rossi vermouth.

Boulevardier

Now, some might say that this only qualifies as a Negroni variant. I don't think so. I think it's a fine cocktail in its own right, and delicious enough to belong on this list. In fact, I even know one or two people who prefer the Boulevardier to the Negroni. Given that my favourite spirit is rye, I understand.

Sazerac

And now for some New Orleans classics. We'll start with the Sazerac. There's nothing better than sipping one while shooting at the Carousel Bar at the Monteleone Hotel, but making them feel at home comes close. The Sazerac would be among my desert island cocktails, were it not for the unfortunate fact that ice is very hard to come by on a desert island.

Vieux Carré

Speaking of the Monteleone, the Vieux Carré (or Old Square, another term for the French quarter) originated at the hotel in 1938. The cocktail mixes rye, cognac, Benedictine and vermouth, along with Peychaud's and Angostura. I've had more than my share at the Carousel Bar, too.

Ramos Gin Fizz

Get out your blender for this one. The Ramos Gin Fizz is a complex drink, made from gin (naturally), lemon and lime juices, simple syrup, orange blossom water, cream, egg white and (optionally) vanilla extract. Traditionally, it has been shaken to hell, first without ice so that the ingredients emulsify, and then with ice so that it becomes extremely cold and frothy. But Gary Regan, a smarter man than me, insists that it's perfectly fine to use a blender for this, so feel free, unless you're trying to tone your arms.

Mint Julep

A few years ago we lived in a flat with backyard access. In addition to grilling, smoking cigars, and enjoying cocktails on the porch, we maintained a garden. One year, mint arrived so abundantly that we ate mint juleps every day for a week. It was a great week.

Whisky Sour

Another easy cocktail to make, the Whiskey Sour requires bourbon or rye, lemon juice and sugar. If you also want a splash of orange juice, I won't stop you. It's a basic drink, of course, but it's part of your arsenal because you'll probably have guests over for a night, and sometimes your guests prefer basic drinks. As long as you have whiskey, lemons and sugar on hand, you can always pull it out.

Mai Tai

My tiki-swilling friends all say, "It's about time you had a tiki drink". Not every bar makes a Mai Tai properly; in fact, it's probably still relatively rare to find one that does, unfortunately. All the more reason to learn how to make them at home. The hardest part is finding everything you need: two rums (preferably, though one will do if it's a dark rum with a rich taste), orange curaçao, and orgeat (try the one from Small Hand Foods.) Shake it all up and strain it over fresh ice. (Heck, you don't even have to do this; I often just dump the entire mixing glass into a cold glass of ice and call it a day).

Planter punch

A lovely, and necessary, drink for summer. Dark rum, lime and lemon, grenadine and simple syrup. Yum. Hell, go crazy and get some umbrellas or fancy straws and be all festive and stuff. Paul Clarke's recipe leaves out the grenadine, you'll notice. I don't know if grenadine is traditional or one of those later additions that piss off the geekiest of geeks. Either way, if you use it, use the DIY stuff, and substitute half of Clarke's simple syrup: so, half ounce simple, half grenadine.

Cosmopolitan

Yes! The Cosmopolitan is on this list! It's a popular drink, so if you throw parties with any regularity, someone will ask you for one. (I made so many at one party, I should have made and bottled them). And you know what? It's a better drink than you think.

The Cosmopolitan is a cultural touchstone because Dale DeGroff once got one in Madonna's hands at the Rainbow Room and it became the drink to be seen with. Then HBO and SJP, of course, made the drink ubiquitous and clichéd. However, sours (like Sidecar, Margaritas and Daiquiri) are staple cocktails, and the Cosmopolitan is, simply put, the best Vodka Sour around.

Pisco Sour

I don't know what else I can say about sours that I haven't already said about the Margarita, the Sidecar and the Whiskey Sour. All I can say is that the pisco version is excellent; the unaged grape spirit is a drink that has a distinct character from its cousins: it is slightly floral and fresh. The addition of an egg white makes the drink creamy and appetising.

Tom Collins

Collinses, historically, are a class of cocktails that require a spirit, a simple syrup, lemon juice and sparkling water. The Tom requires gin, of course. Historically, this would have been Old Tom gin, hence the name, but nowadays dry London is common. Try it with Old Tom, if you have it, though. Or sub in the spirit of your choice; anything will work in this formula. This drink is so refreshing and so easy to sip that I think anyone who loves to drink should be able to make one.

Yes, yes, you can skimp and pour the gin into a glass and fill it with Sprite. The first time I was intoxicated was in a Sprite version of Tom Collins at a cousin's wedding when I was in high school. I have a soft spot for these Collins knockoffs, but I still urge you not to do it this way. The drink is much more delicious, made with fresh, real juice.

Last word

What a story this drink has! If this were the story of a forgotten boxer, rediscovered years later by a fight fan, Clint Eastwood would have directed the film by now. The drink originated in Detroit during Prohibition, but fell into oblivion for decades until it was rediscovered by Murray Stenson in Seattle. The Last Word is a complex, herbaceous drink, and like the French 75, it's a drink that I think would make anyone a gin lover.

Tips And Tricks From The Masters Of Mixology

Being a bartender today means that you have to be skilled at making drinks, know all styles of cocktails and follow the trends and tastes of contemporary drinks.

Speed counts behind the bar, and you have to be personable: guests are not just there for a good drink, they want to have fun too. How do you get and stay at the top of your bartending game? We asked several professionals for some advice; here are 13 tips.

Educate yourself on the basics

Read books and watch technical videos online, says Dimitrios Zahariadis, co-founder of TheCocktailChemist.com and president of the U.S. Bartenders Guild Connecticut Chapter (USBG CT).

As for recommended reading, New York bartender Jon Kraus swears by The Bar Book: Elements of Cocktail Technique, by Jeffrey Morgenthaler; Liquid Intelligence: The Art and Science of the Perfect Cocktail, by Dave

Arnold; and the Bartender's Choice app by Sam Ross of Milk & Honey.

"Definitely buy The Mr. Boston Official Bartender's Guide," says James Menite, bartender at The Plaza Hotel in New York. "When I first started, I got so into that book. Now one of my recipes is in the book. My career has come full circle." He finds time to work both in the kitchen and behind the bar.

"It teaches you to be fast, clean and organised," says bar consultant Johan M. Stein, director of Cat & Mouse Consulting. Barbacking is also great for young bartenders, he notes. "I became a very good bartender because I was a good bartender before and I proved myself."

Practice mise en place or 'putting in place'.

Organize and arrange the items you expect to use during a shift for easy access to save time, says Joe Alberti, bartender at McCoy's Oceanfront at the Fort Lauderdale Marriott Pompano Beach Resort & Spa.

Make your own syrups

Homemade syrups not only add a fresh element that can't be bought in shops, "but they also save money, as they last about a week and are only the cost of a cup of sugar and things like an inch of ginger or a pineapple," says Cody Goldstein, head bartender at Red Farm in New York.

It's a good idea to infuse simple syrups with herbs, fruit, etc. rather than infusing alcohol, says Alberti. This reduces liquor waste.

Use a jigger.

Measuring with a jigger provides quality control and allows you to get exact proportions every time you make a cocktail, says Chris Almeida, bartender at The Eddy in Providence, RI, and president of USBG Rhode Island. "You can make the cocktail exactly the same way, every time. It eliminates a lot of variable factors," he says. "Friends don't let friends not use jiggers."

Learn to pour freely.

While many recommend using a jigger for most pours, bartenders should also be able to pour freely. Practice every day to learn how to pour 0.5 to 0.5 grams at a time with both hands, says Zachary Blair, lead mixologist at Whiteface Lodge in Lake Placid, NY. You should also learn how to pour, keep pouring from one glass to another, he says.

Aim to get the right pour every time, says Owen Joseph, bar supervisor at the Sea Crest Beach Hotel on Cape Cod, MA. "You're sure it's going to be a great drink, and your guests will always have a consistent one."

Count as you pour and adjust your count by ounces or parts thereof."

Use a glassware rimming plate.

Don't dip glass rims for sugar and salt into typical plastic containers, Alberti says. Instead, use a plate so the salt or sugar doesn't get into the glass and create an unbalanced cocktail.

Get local ingredients.

Visit local farmers' markets, gardens, and even florists, says Greg Fournier, beverage director at the Harbor View Hotel on Martha's Vineyard. "Everyone loves the sweet floral scents in the summer and the complex, unique flavors of herbs for fall."

And if you don't know what's at the farmer's markets, just ask, says Bob Peters, head mixologist at The Punch Room at the Ritz-Carlton in Charlotte, NC. "Most of the time the farmers are more than happy to let you taste their fresh produce."

Always clean the cans after every drink.

"I've worked with numerous bartenders who throw their cans in the sink after every drink," says Goldstein. "This not only leaves them without cans at some point, but it slows down the process during work hours if they have to make more than one drink at a time."

Use a mixed spray bottle to mimic a rinsing technique.

It's quicker to spray the spirit from the Misto bottle into a glass than to pour a small amount, coat the inside of the glass and then drain off the excess, says Peters. This also eliminates waste "and will extend the life of a bottle three to four times longer than if using a traditional rinsing technique".

In addition, spray rinsing can be a beautiful and interesting part of your beverage presentation, notes Peters. "Spraying vermouth or absinthe in a glass in front of your guests really piques their interest and can start a dialogue that will make for a unique experience that can be truly memorable."

Develop your signature shake.

Have fun when shaking a drink: 'It's one of the most important parts of bartending because it makes the spirit softer with dilution and customers love it,' says Blair of Whiteface Lodge.

Every bartender has their own shake, so don't be afraid to get creative. But be sure to count the shakes and make them the same every time, Blair notes. "The more or less a drink is shaken determines the consistency of the cocktail, which ultimately brings people back to the bar."

Making a complex drink in batches.

Some state laws prevent bartenders from pouring their own drinks, so split the alcohol from the mix, Blair says. Instead of adding each ingredient at a time, make a large batch and put it in a bottle.

"The mix should easily fit in a quart container and it makes it super easy when the mixer is out," Blair says. Just get a funnel, fill the bottle and keep pouring. The ration for this type of pre-packaged cocktail is roughly one part spirit to two parts mixer, he adds.

Smile and be friendly.

Keep a few interesting stories and jokes in your pocket to make conversation with guests, says Labinot Gashi, bartender at the Gaby Bar at Sofitel New York.

Remember that "you don't serve people drinks, you serve drinks to people," says Sabrine Dhaliwal, bar manager, West Restaurant + Bar, Vancouver, BC. Women tend to have a certain touch and finesse that men don't, she says, so if you're a female bartender, "be proud, be yourself and work hard." And there's not much that can beat a woman's smile.

Remember your regular customers.

Always remember what your regulars like to drink, says Gashi. It will keep them coming back.

And when you find yourself serving returning customers, ask them if they want their usual, instead of the name of the cocktail, adds Gashi. This makes the guests feel good: they've found someone who listens to them.

The Essential Tool Kit

Being an experienced bartender is more than just casually mixing drinks for your friends at home. It's an art form that requires practice, skill and care.

But even the most dedicated bartenders would be nothing without their essential bar tools to help them along the way. Without these tools, bartenders would be pouring mixed drinks between two red solo glasses until it seemed mixed enough.

Bar tools are to bartenders what a paintbrush is to an artist. Here are the 10 essential tools every bartender should have if they want to be a master mixer.

It doesn't matter if you're bartending at a party, or if you want to turn mixing drinks into a career, you don't want to look like an amateur. Here are 10 essential bartending tools that will make you look like an expert mixologist from the start.

1. Cocktail Shaker

This is the pinnacle of all bar tools. Without a cocktail shaker, you're basically a first-year college student mixing drinks in plastic cups in your dorm room. Take the first step to becoming a real bartender and buy a shaker.

Your shaker will be your most used bar tool when it comes to creating mixed drinks. Make sure you get one that is easy to use and durable. You will learn that having a quality cocktail shaker is the first step to becoming a good bartender.

2. Measuring instrument

You will need a measuring instrument so that you can measure the quantities of each ingredient in your drink. You can use a basic measuring cup like the one you have at home, or you can get a measuring instrument specially made for mixing drinks, such as a jigger.

Getting the right ingredients in each drink is the most important part of creating a quality drink. You need to have the perfect amount of strength, sweetness and acidity in each drink.

Don't fixate on the amount of each ingredient, especially when you are just starting out. Use a measuring device to make sure you get the right ingredients.

3. Bar spoons

Bar spoons are a necessary tool for drinks that need to be stirred rather than shaken. You can use a normal spoon, but these are generally too bulky for many drinks, especially if the drink is in a martini glass. Bar spoons are longer and narrower than regular spoons. They make it super easy to mix any kind of drink, no matter what kind of glass it's in.

4. Drink strainer

A strainer is a necessary addition to your cocktail shaker. If you are shaking a mixed drink with fruit, ice, herbs or anything other than liquid, you will need a strainer.

The strainer can be attached to your cocktail mixer so that when you pour the contents of the mixer into glasses, it will catch anything that is not liquid. Without a strainer, your drinks will all be filled with small chunks of whatever you mixed.

5. Personalised bottle opener

A bartender doesn't just mix drinks. You also need to know how to serve a beer. Many times people will want beer on tap. But many people will also ask for it by the bottle, especially if you have unique bottles of beer.

For these cases, make sure you have a cool, custom bottle opener. Instead of opting for a generic bottle opener, you can show a little bit of your personality and get something unique for your bar.

6. Grater

Take your bartending game up a notch and get a grater. You can grate all kinds of fun ingredients into your drinks to give them an extra boost of flavour. The grater can be used for spices and herbs such as fresh ginger, or for citrus fruits such as lemon or orange. Adding these grated features can take your mixed drinks to the next level.

7. Mixing glass

A cocktail glass is a durable glass that is used to mix drinks before serving them to customers. Cocktail glasses can stay cold for much longer than a normal glass, which is great for serving cold drinks without ice.

8. Citrus juicer

Using fresh citrus juice in your drinks instead of pre-bottled juices is a great step towards becoming a good bartender. All you need is the fruit of your choice, such as lemon or lime, and a good citrus juicer.

Cut up the desired amount of citrus fruit and put it in the juicer. Squeeze the juice into your blender to provide a fresh addition to your mixed drink.

9. Pocket knife

A small knife is a simple but vital addition to your bar tools. You can use it to cut citrus segments, chop herbs and spices, or create twists for garnishing drinks.

You don't need a big chef's knife for these things. All you need is a small, sharp knife that you feel comfortable using.

10. Pouring spout
Spouts are essential for bartenders if you want to create a drink efficiently, accurately and without making a mess. You should use a spout for all the liquor you pour in order to avoid wasting time and looking like an amateur.

All you have to do is twist the spout on top of the liquor bottle and you will be able to pour a smooth drink for your friends or customers.

THE ART OF SMOKING COCKTAILS

• •

For some, it is the scent of smoked bacon for garnish. For others, it's the seductive white vapour dancing like a genie from his stone glass. With so many evocative, pendant-flavoured libations appearing on menus, many cocktail enthusiasts have experienced that existential moment: How did our cocktails get so smoky?

Let's start with the more recent side of the story. The smoking trend began in 2007, when New York bartender Eben Freeman conjured up the much-loved Waylon, a mix of smoked Coke and bourbon. It was a slow start, but since then the ingredients of the smoked cocktail have made a comeback. Smoked ice and table salt. Tobacco-infused syrup. Smoked teas, tinctures and herbs (including, yes, that herb). Nearly every standard recipe basked in the smoky spotlight, from martinis and Bloody Marys to Old Fashioneds and margaritas, plus seasonal creations from beverage directors across the country.

Smokers and mini blowtorches are the best modern bar tools. But whisky expert Dave Broom (author of World Atlas of Whisky and Whisky: The Manual) reminds us that the roots of liquid smoking began a long time ago, mostly with two key spirits: Scotch whisky and Oaxaca mezcal. The distinctive flavours inherent in each stem from the production process, where the raw materials, barley and agave respectively, get the slow roasting treatment.

Early Origins

"From a surprisingly early age," says Broom, "peat has been used for quality reasons." Brown and soil-like, peat beds take thousands of years to form, consisting of decomposed moss and plant matter. Centuries before peat became a popular garden soil, top scientists celebrated it as the best fuel for malting and encouraged its use to dry barley. The phenols released in the burning peat create oils in the smoke that help form the character of the whisky.

With mezcal, the peat and the kiln are replaced by a huge underground kiln, or fire pit. And agave. A lot of agave.

Dr Iván Saldaña Oyarzábal runs the website The Anatomy of Mezcal, has a PhD in biochemistry and founded Montelobos Mezcal. In Oaxaca, where 93% of mezcal is produced, traditional methods dictate that large fire pits are heated with hardwood (pine or Mexican oak) covered with volcanic rocks. "The rocks absorb so much heat that they will eventually look red and orange," says Saldaña. The smoke released during the four-day cooking process gives the spirit its spicy, chocolatey notes.

For both whisky and mezcal, smoke can be crucial, but it doesn't deserve all the credit. And although it is used extensively, 'smoke' is not an all-encompassing term. What makes a smoky whisky work well is "everything around the cloudiness," says Broom. "Smoke always has a drying effect in the mouth." For a smoked whisky to be balanced, you need sweetness." That's where the rest of the production-fermentation, the distillation, comes in.

Similarly, Saldaña recognises the role that agave and fermentation play in the creation of a mezcal blanco like the one produced in Montelobos. The green agave contributes bright, citrusy notes, thanks to the raw elements that survive the cooking process. The cooked agave offers a rounder, more caramelised flavour. The yeast produced during fermentation gives off a ripe, fruity aroma. The intensity and flavour of the smoke in a given mezcal can change depending on the type of wood used in the fire, how dry or wet it is, the proportions of wood to agave and the cooking time.

Broom says that over time the palate of human beings has developed to actually crave smoke. Most cultures have dishes that focus on grilling or barbecuing. If drinks are largely driven by the food we eat, it's no wonder we've found ways to activate those senses in liquid form. However, anyone who has taken a dip in the smoke at their favourite cocktail bar knows that a little smoke is good for you. With smoke, you can definitely have too much of a good thing.

Bartenders would do well to "study smoked spirits for themselves," says Broom. "With a little smoky booze, the smoke appears immediately." Others, you pick it up in the middle of the palate."

Saldaña warns that the smokiness of mezcal can be difficult to predict once mixed into a cocktail. The culprit is dilution. "Smoke is relative on the matrix of alcohol and water," says the biochemist-distiller. "You can have a mezcal at 45 degrees, with a nice, balanced smoke." But when you mix that product and the alcohol is reduced, suddenly the smoke is screaming in your face."

That's why it's so common to see cocktails use a tequila-mezcal mash-up: The bartender tries to control for the mezcal's dragon breath. "The spirit-smoke integration is the job of the master distiller," Saldaña continues. "If they've done their job right, a bartender should be able to use mezcal as a base spirit."

Both Broom and Saldaña have indicated that they prefer their smoke to be intrinsic to the spirit. But why should mezcal and scotch have all the fun?

Trevor Frye, beverage director at Jack Rose Dining Saloon in Washington, D.C. and his small cocktail bar

Dram + Grain, uses a smoking gun for his Ode to Omaha. The rum-based drink is a nod to Nebraska's Berry & Rye bar, where he and his friend began experimenting with smoking. There were challenges.

"We thought smoky drinks were interesting, but in general they weren't executed well. The smoke was either overpowering to the palate, or it was just for show."

The Ode to Omaha, similar to an Old Fashioned rum, has a lot of fanfare, admits Frye. But it is "a work of art with a purpose". Using wood shavings and a dry smoker, Frye directs a tube of smoke into a glass container of Thomas Tew Rum, fruit-based syrup, and Jerry Thomas bitters, stopping it with a cork. "The smoke mixes well with the rum, and plays with the woody spice of the rum," says Frye.

The Smoky Future

Although there are some differences in the production of mezcal, Saldaña says there are currently no major variations in the firing process. With whisky, on the other hand, Broom has taken note of several distillers who proudly describe their product as a "non-scotch" option. They have incorporated the terroir of their country into the malting process, so the flavours of the whisky depend on the raw materials used to smoke the barley.

In Denmark, Fary Lochan uses nettles, which give the whisky a grassy, herbal flavour. Flóki, an Icelandic single malt, smokes barley with sheep dung. "The sample I had was only five years old, but it was quite agricultural and herbal," recalls Broom. Down in Australia, Lark Distillery uses a peat that reminded Broom of eucalyptus, a clean, woody flavour. A future as dense and hazy as this has never seemed brighter.

The Charm Of Smoke

Although cocktails may seem a little strange, the use of smoke to add complexity to drinks goes back almost to the roots of the craft cocktail movement. Like many other experiments, it was taken to the logical extreme: bartenders smoked virtually every ingredient behind the bar.

According to master mixologist Jim Meehan, this is probably an evolution of the barbecue trend in the food world. Because it may be a new flavour for bartenders, it may also be the next logical step for bartenders who have experimented with more traditional flavour combinations.

Despite its modern appeal, it is likely that humans have had to evolve to enjoy the taste of smoke, even though we are not actually able to taste it; humans do not have specific receptors in our taste buds for smokiness. Fortunately for us, the taste of a food or drink comes from three sources: smell, taste and physical reactions (such as the texture or heat of a chilli pepper). For smoke, almost all of its flavour comes from its characteristic smell.

Since smell triggers memories more than any other sense, our associations between smoke and summer barbecues or nights spent camping make it an interesting ingredient to play with.

Charred Cocktails

There are two ways to add smoke to a drink: either infusing it with smoke, or simply using a smoky ingredient. Nowadays, there are many ways to infuse a cocktail with smoke. Tutorials abound for smoking ice on the grill or infusing a whole drink with a Smoking Gun. Dedicated products like Liquid Smoke also make it easy to instantly add char with just a few drops.

The craft cocktail movement has also spawned a myriad of smoky ingredients. From smoked salmon vodka to walnut liqueur, the world of spirits is awash with new smoke. But two liqueurs, Scotch whisky and mezcal, retain the distinction as smoky originals.

Scotch is one of the most polarising categories on the market. While it may be mild and malty, it is best known for being earthy and smoky. But this distinctive flavour does not come from water or the distillation process. On the contrary, the smoke is impregnated in advance.

After the barley used to make scotch has been obtained, it is soaked to begin the germination process. To prevent germination, the grain is heated, completing the process known as malting. As peat, commonly available in Scotland, is an excellent fuel, it is often used to fuel the fire. The more peat used, the smokier the resulting whisky.

Mezcal, which is often described as a spicy, smoky tequila, is produced rather differently. This Mexican staple is produced by cooking agave hearts in an underground oven. By lining these ovens with volcanic rocks and heating the hearts over an open flame, this multi-day process smokes and caramelises the agave while cooking it.

Unlike the infusion of partial or whole cocktails, the use of smoked ingredients presents a number of unique challenges. Firstly, cocktail preparation normally requires dilution. Dilution of any spirit lowers the alcohol content. It also releases new flavour compounds while masking others, which changes the flavour of the alcohol. As a result, a light and fuzzy Scotch or mezcal can become a one-note smoke bomb when mixed in a cocktail. In addition, Scotch and some mezcals have a reputation for being liqueurs that drink themselves. Some purists may shy away from these cocktails, but that means more for us.

Despite the risks, bartenders over the centuries have strived to perfect drinks with smoky ingredients. Classics like the suave Rob Roy and the curious Blood & Sand are now joined by modern smoky cocktails. Be sure to ask your bartender for guidance if you're in the mood for a little smoke.

New School vs. Old School

Striking a balance between adding a depth of flavour to your cocktails, while creating theatre and that perfect photogenic moment, is something you really want to achieve. While creating a buzz on social media can be beneficial, the quality and consistency of your bar menu is something that should be at the forefront of your mind.

As a first step, it's important to find the right drink to smoke. Traditionally, the richest cocktails, with dark, heady spits like whisky, brandy or rum, result in wonderful campfire notes that you get from smoking.

Some drinks are simply not enhanced by the smoking process. There no exact right or wrong, but drinks that are great for their flavour and fresh sheen are likely to be dulled by the hot smoke of charred wood chips or spices. Trial and error (and a good dose of common sense) will take you a long way when experimenting with cocktail smoke.

The New School

The easiest way to inject smoke into a cocktail is to use a professional smoking machine. Today, the best option is to use a smoking gun. A smoking gun is realistically just a portable vacuum cleaner that contains wood shavings.

These shavings are then lit on fire with a lighter or a blowtorch, with the vacuum pulling the resulting smoke through a hose and out the end nozzle. This nozzle can be placed inside bottles, glass objects or even a smoke box.

Smoke boxes work by placing the desired finished cocktail in a small glass box, filling the box with the desired level of smoke and releasing the drink to your guest through a glass door, an effect that can be so impressive.

Old-Fashioned Smoking

Alternatively, there are easier and cheaper ways to inject smoke into your creations. Take, for example, a classic Sazerac... Traditionally you simply add rye whisky, sugar and bitters to a cocktail glass, stir for 20 seconds, then strain into a glass with an absinthe rinse. Absinthe adds an herbal, almost minty aroma to the drink, adding depth and a curious finish to an old-fashioned.

A simple alternative to this would be to take a bunch of anise-like herbs such as tarragon or fennel tips, dry them and place them on a wooden cutting board. These dried herbs are then sprinkled with a few dashes of absinthe and set alight. Follow by taking your glass of stone that fits the burnt leaves and let the lack of oxygen extinguish the cocktail and release the smoke. At this point you move on to the normal Sazerac operating procedure, creating the rest of the drink. Once ready, strain the mixture into the glass filled with eucalyptus-smoke for a simple smoke-filled alternative.

Whether it's dried aromatic leaves, spices like cinnamon or cardamom, or more traditional wood shavings, adding smoke to cocktails can be as easy as finding the right aromatic, burning it and letting the fire aromatics fill a glass.

Once you have set up the equipment and the drink, decide which element of your drink to smoke, whether the liquid itself, the serving vessel, or the garnish, as well as how much smoke to inject into the drink. These decisions can make or break your drink. A lighter cocktail such as a Martini may only need a gesture of a smoked olive to have an effect, while other drinks such as Penicillin or Bloody Mary can probably withstand marinating the entire drink in a box full of applewood smoke for twenty or thirty seconds. Trial and error is the key to mastering the art of smoking cocktails.

Why not try it?

5 Golden Rules

- Not all drinks can be enhanced by smoking cocktails.
- Smoke dark, intoxicating cocktails such as whisky, brandy or rum.
- A smoking gun is the easiest and most professional way to put smoke into cocktails.
- Decide whether to smoke the liquid, serve the vessel or garnish.
- Trial and error is the key to mastering the art of cocktail smoking.

MAKING (SUPERB) SMOKY DRINKS

• •

F ire and smoke are awesome no matter what, but when those fireworks translate into delicious drinks, it's really something now. While bartenders have been smoking drinks for years, it's not just for professionals anymore. There are a couple of ways to smoke ingredients and cocktails at home, and both are pretty easy. It just takes a little time, the right equipment (there's that excuse you've been looking for to buy a smoking gun) and a fire extinguisher nearby, just in case.

If you really want to impress someone, there's nothing better than starting a fire. And when it comes to smoked cocktails, the effect is much more of a presentation - though it's certainly Instagram-worthy.

"The aromatic qualities of the smoke add a dryness that is more of a perception than a reduction in sugar. You also get more tannic qualities from the wood," explains Ben Potts, bar manager and owner of Miami's Beaker & Gray.

And of course there's the smell of whatever you're smoking, which helps to enrich the drink. "The aroma excites the palate and adds depth to the flavour of the cocktail," says Norton Christopher, bar chef at Sac-a-Lait in New Orleans.

Add it all up, and the smoke adds a multi-sensory experience to the cocktail - one that can be done at home, with the right equipment and some safety precautions (since you're working with fire and alcohol, after all). Follow these pro tips to create rich, smoky whisky cocktails.

Technique & Equipment

There's more than one way to smoke a cocktail, depending on how much you want to invest and how much smoke you want to add, says Potts, who often experiments with smoked cocktails and puts them on the menu at Beaker & Grey.

The first option, which will give the smokiest flavour, is to rinse the glass with smoke. First, cool the glass. "Smoke tends to stick to things that are cold," says Potts. Make the cocktail and, just before pouring, take what you're smoking and light it on fire, preferably with a blowtorch. Do not use lighter fluid, as it will give a chemical taste. Turn your chilled glass upside down over the burning ingredient (options below), covering it completely, and the smoke will stick to the sides of the glass. Once the smoke dissipates, you are ready to pour.

Another option is to rinse the entire cocktail with smoke. Use a large container such as a wine decanter or a jug with a small opening to catch the smoke. As above, after cooling the vessel, set fire to the smoking ingredient, then put the vessel on top. Leave some oxygen in this way, the fire will burn longer and you will be able to collect as much smoke as possible. Once you are satisfied with your smoke (a few minutes is a good rule of thumb), pour your prepared cocktail into the pot and swirl it around. You can leave it to rest, but most of the smoke flavour will occur in the first 30 seconds or so. Pour your smoky drink into a glass and enjoy.

If you plan to make smoked cocktails your speciality, consider buying a smoking gun. You can find one on Amazon for about $100. Place the smoking ingredient in the top chamber and use the tube to pour a controlled stream of smoke directly into the glass.

The last option creates the most intense flavour, but requires extreme caution. If you have a smoker or grill, create a smoky fire with the same wood shavings or boards you would use for meat. Make a double boiler: put the liquid you want to smoke in one pot or heatproof bowl, and put it in another pot or bowl filled with ice (this way the liquid will not heat up, which will change the taste). Place the double boiler outside the flame where it is cooler, but can still catch smoke.

SAFETY
I don't need to tell you that fire and alcohol can be a dangerous combination. Use common sense if you decide to make smoked cocktails. Don't wear baggy clothes and tie back long hair. Consider smoking your drinks outdoors if you use a smoking gun. And if you've already had a few smoked Manhattans, it's safer to prepare an unsmoked cocktail for the next round.

INGREDIENTS
There are many ingredients you can use to create smoked cocktails, and Potts encourages experimentation. "You don't know what something is going to smell like when it's smoked unless you pull out the matchbox," he says. While developing a particular

cocktail, he smoked 10 or 15 different ingredients until he found the one with the perfect aromatic qualities for that drink. "Light something on the fire, smell the smoke and if it smells good, try rinsing the glass with the smoke," he says. "If you like it, then try rinsing the cocktail with smoke in a larger container."

Here are some ingredients to try, each of which lends a specific flavour to your cocktail:

- Oak wood: can partially mimic barrel ageing and accentuate the charred wood notes in whisky
- Pecan wood: charred nuts
- Rosemary: rustic, herbaceous flavour
- Cinnamon: subtle sweetness and lighter smoke
- Vanilla beans: sweet and light smoke
- Citrus peel: use as a garnish to provide the essence over the cocktail
- Salt: can lift a drink and enhance the full flavour profile
- Ice: creates a gradual, subtle smokiness as it melts (For full instructions on creating smoked ice, see the recipe for Smoked Old Fashioned).

You can also treat things you smoke with added flavours. Try chocolate bitters over wood chips, or dip what you plan to burn in absinthe, rum, peppery scotch or other highly flammable, flavoured liquids.

Top Smoke And Whisky Combinations

If you're a little shy about playing mad scientist with your cocktails, try these flavour combinations, which tend to work well together. Keep in mind that smoke works best for blended cocktails.

- Rye with any wood: "The spicy nature of rye works really well with oak, cherry or walnut," says Potts, adding that a smoked Manhattan is a good smoked cocktail to start with.

- Bourbon with corn husks: "The corn husks accentuate the corn in the bourbon while providing a slight sweetness," says Christopher.

- Scotch with thyme: "Even without smoking, thyme has a smoky characteristic, and scotch always works well with smoky things, even if it's not peated," says Potts.

- Wheat Bourbon with cinnamon: Because Bourbon is sweet, the sweet notes of cinnamon will complement it, according to Potts.

- Irish whiskey with coffee beans: "When I'm still drinking Irish whiskey in the pot, the most prevalent notes are coffee and chocolate," says Potts. "It would be interesting to enrich it with coffee or even coffee beans dusted with cocoa powder."

- Japanese whisky with citrus peel: Lighter Japanese whisky needs a delicate smoke that is not overpowering, plus citrus peel enhances the fruity notes of the whisky.

- Corn whisky with pecan wood: 'The nutty pecan wood really shines with corn whisky, providing a balance of sweet and savoury characteristics,' says Christopher.

The Presentation

Part of the fun of smoking cocktails is the presentation. Bring the glass to a heat-proof table or tray with the ingredients already burnt, so your guests can watch the swirl of smoke. Then turn the glass upside down and pour the drink.

You can also use smoked ingredients, such as cinnamon sticks and herbs, as a garnish. "At Sac-a-Lait we serve a cocktail called Gettin Figgy Wit It," says Christopher. "I don't include any kind of smoke in the actual cocktail." Instead, I incinerate a sprig of rosemary as a garnish." When the guest receives the drink, the sprig is still smoking. This adds a slight smokiness to the cocktail and is designed to create a good aroma".

THE RIGHT TIPS FOR A PERFECT SMOKED COCKTAIL

Smoking is a technique of preserving and flavouring food (in the broadest sense of the term) by exposing it to smoke generated by burning wood or other substances of plant origin (dry spices, tea, etc.). Probably discovered by accident by cavemen, this process has been used for many centuries to preserve mainly meat and fish. The smoke obtained by burning the wood is rich in substances such as formaldehyde, acetic acid and some phenolic compounds that are powerful antimicrobials and antioxidants. Nowadays, it is still used for this purpose but, as more effective preservation and faster transport methods have been discovered, flavouring is certainly the most interesting result and this is what we will focus on.

Cellulose and hemicellulose are composed of sugars, while lignin is one of the most complex substances in nature and consists of phenolic compounds. The higher the amount of lignin, the harder the wood and the higher the combustion temperature. During combustion, the various components of the wood are transformed into other compounds, some of which are responsible for the aromatic profile of the food or drink after contact with the smoke. The sugars contained in cellulose and hemicellulose, burning between 200 and 320 °C, are transformed into molecules which can contain fruity (lactones and acetaldehyde), oreal, bread crust (furans) or buttery (diacetyl) notes. Burning the lignin (ideal temperature 400 °C), on the other hand, releases vanillin, phenols with a smoky, pungent note and eugenol with a clove-like aroma.

The type of wood and the combustion temperature are two very important factors in achieving a pleasant flavour. Oak, walnut and fruit trees produce a balanced smoke as opposed to pine, fir and conifers which are too rich in resin. As far as temperature is concerned, 400°C is the maximum value above which the molecules produced risk losing their aromatic charge or becoming unpleasant. For the sake of completeness, it should be remembered that during combustion, substances such as benzo(a)pyrene and other polycyclic aromatic hydrocarbons are also generated, which may be harmful to health in the long term. This is another reason why it is important to limit the combustion temperature.

Smoked drinks are certainly nothing new in the bar and have been tried and tested extensively. There are various techniques for smoking drinks, which are more or less complex. The most immediate and simple method is to use smoked spirits in the creation or interpretation of a drink. Peated Scotch Whiskies or Mezcal, if dosed correctly, are excellent in this respect. For convenience, a plastic perfume atomiser can also be used to spray the product into the drink. Another strategy is to use liquid smoke. The basis of this additive is water, which is flavoured with smoke. There are different flavours available on the market. Before use, it is best to read the label and check whether there is a maximum dose that can be administered, even though it is generally safer than a 'do-it-yourself' smoke. Liquid smoke must in fact respect threshold values for certain potentially harmful substances present in it (Legislative Decree No 107 of 25 January 1992, Annex III). The most commonly used procedure involves putting the drink directly in contact with the smoke produced by a portable smoker (smoking gun or aladdin). Many bartenders, after mixing the drink, place it in a glass bell filled with smoke and leave it in contact with the gas for a few tens of seconds.

Using the smoking gun in this way is certainly very choreographic, but the drink will not have a uniform and pleasant smoke: only part of the drink will be flavoured but it could also be over-smoked.

Much more functional would be to prepare the drink in a mixin' glass, fill a bottle with the desired smoke, pour the cocktail into the bottle, shake the bottle and immediately pour it into a glass with ice (Jamie Boudreau, How to smoke a cocktail). Better still would be to flavour just the ice and then use it to dilute the drink. Smoking only the ice would require less smoke for the benefit of customers who might not like the smell that would waft through the room.

SMOKED COCKTAIL RECIPES

· ·

S moke is not just for grilling. Bartenders have started experimenting with the stuff for cocktail programmes, resulting in unique layered drinks with a seductive smoky note.

You can use an expensive smoking gun, which allows you to channel smoke from charred wood chips (or any other easily burned aromatics, such as tea or herbs) through a tube and into a glass. We think it is easier, however, to use a hand torch and a wooden board.

You use the torch to char the board, then hold a jar over the burnt area to catch the smoke. When you have enough, pour in your cocktail, add a lid to the jar, swirl it around for about 30 seconds and boom: a perfectly smoked cocktail. It's easy, it tastes good, and it's almost guaranteed to impress your drinking buddy.

You also have a few different options on what you want to smoke. You can:

● **Smoke a cocktail.** Simply mix what you want to smoke and then pour it into the jar full of smoke.

- **Smoke the spirit.** This is good if you want to add a unique note to something that otherwise wouldn't taste like smoke, like gin or tequila. Then you can sip it neat, or use that pre-smoked spirit to mix into a cocktail for more subtle results.

- **Smoke the ice cubes.** Seriously. They play a surprisingly important role in the quality of a cocktail, and we've seen top bars smoke ice before serving a drink. It gives a very subtle smokiness that is noticeable, but not overwhelming.

You can also burn aromatics such as loose-leaf tea, rosemary or dried spices to add a bit of variety. If you are using a torch, simply place the aromatics in a small pile on the table, char them and capture the resulting smoke.

Once you have all that, you just have to choose the drink you want to smoke. Anything will work, really, but we recommend alcoholic drinks with few ingredients. This is because the nuances of a drink that uses a large amount of ingredients can quickly get lost once smoke enters the equation, so it's best to stick to simpler recipes with assertive flavours that can punch back. Try one of these:

Smoked Maple Old Fashioned

My current mission is to make sure that smoked maple desserts and recipes are tested regularly. Let's start with this old-fashioned smoked maple and it's so perfect for the season. Smoky. Flavourful. And warming. How it warms you to the core. And really good. A fortnight ago I went to an event at DeLallo and they had this Knob Creek maple bourbon whiskey smoked. Oh God.

I know I'm ranting about my weird love of maple (I haven't been interested in it my whole life!) and the moment I saw it I almost died. I tasted it that night and then, when I had to make a wine run for a party a week later, I grabbed a bottle. I am... obsessed. YES. I knew old-fashioned smoked maple had to happen.

This is super smoky. Super maple. It's really delicious and I know I wanted to create some sort of fun cocktail with it! We did our own little version of smoking a slice of lemon and orange zest in a glass before adding the bitters, maple syrup and smoked maple bourbon. It definitely boosted the smoky flavour and made it so interesting. If you like bourbon and you also like smoky cocktails (think: mezcal!) then you will go crazy for this.

It packs a powerful punch. It's worth it!

While I usually only do punch and sangria (they're definitely the easiest for a crowd!), these really only take a few minutes to put together. Especially if you have everything ready to go. They'd be perfect for a small Thanksgiving gathering - before or after dinner.

The best part? If you're a crazy autumn fanatic like me, and you wait all year for crisp leaves and cold air and bonfires and hay rides, this is the best part. It tastes of all these things right in a glass. Live for it.

INGREDIENTS

- 1 spiral of lemon peel
- 1/2 ounce of maple syrup
- 2 to 3 drops angostura bitters
- 2 to 3 ounces of maple-smoked bourbon whisky
- cinnamon stick if desired

INSTRUCTIONS

1. Use a kitchen torch to light the lemon or orange peel and place it in a glass, covering the top for a minute or two. Remove the zest, run it around the rim of the glass and add an ice cube.

2. Add a few drops of bitters, then add the maple syrup. Add the bourbon. Stir, add the cinnamon stick and serve.

Smoked Whiskey Apple Cider

There's a little part of me, the size of a pinky finger, that wishes I was a shrewish writer. That I could wear the dark wood office look, don a smoking jacket and pull out brown booze every time writer's block kicks in. But that's not my life (because I'm not a man, nor am I a great writer, nor do I live in the 1950s) and so I channel desires into cocktails like this Smoked Whiskey Apple Cider.

When the weather cools down, I want a drink that will warm me from the inside out and keep me going regardless of the temperature and, let's be honest, nothing helps more than a shot of good liquor. Nothing except a spiced and flavoured apple cider with the smoky taste of lapsang souchong tea. It's a smoky tea that's too much for me on its own, but it's a big hit in a drink like this.

Ingredients

- 8 cups unfiltered apple cider
- 1 Fuji apple
- 4 whole cloves
- 2 whole cinnamon sticks
- 1 sliced medium orange
- 1/4 cup honey
- 2 1/2 tablespoons lapsang souchong smoked tea (about 6 tea bags)
- 1 cup aged rum, whisky or bourbon

Instructions

1. Boil apple cider over low heat: Fill a medium saucepan with apple cider, apple, cloves, cinnamon sticks, orange slices and honey and bring to a boil over high heat. Reduce heat to a simmer, cover and allow cinnamon and cloves to stir until desired strength is reached, about 10-15 minutes.

2. Add the smoked tea and serve: Remove the lid, raise the heat and bring back to the boil. Once the boil is reached, stir in the lapsang souchong tea, reduce the heat to a simmer and let steep until the desired strength is reached, about 4-6 minutes.

Strain the mixture, stir in the alcohol and place in mugs or allow to cool completely and store in an airtight container in the refrigerator. Serve warm.

Smoky Mezcal Negroni

This smoked cocktail is a twist on the classic negroni. Made with smoked simple syrup and mezcal it's the perfect smoky cocktail for cocktail parties.

Since there are only 3 ingredients, the negroni is open to endless experimentation. Sub bourbon for the gin and you have a boulevardier. Sub prosecco for the vermouth and you have a sbagliatto. The list goes on and on.

As a cocktail expert, brands sometimes send me samples of high quality spirits. One brand sent me some very fine tequila reposado. Naturally, as I am a big fan of negronis, I decided to make a tequila negroni.

What is Mezcal?

Later that week, my cousin (aka Mr. Hyde) was moving, so he gave me most of his liquor, including a bottle of mezcal. In a nutshell, mezcal is a liquor made from distilled agave. But so is tequila. So what's the difference between tequila and mezcal?

Here's the skinny: mezcal is defined as any agave-based liqueur, which is a very broad umbrella. Tequila is only considered tequila if it is made from blue agave, and just as champagne can only come from the Champagne region of France, tequila can only come from the Mexican city of Tequila and its surroundings.

Mezcal has a noticeably smokier taste than tequila, and this smokiness comes from a process in which the piñas (or hearts of the agave plant) are slowly roasted in an underground pit for about 3 days. They are then crushed and left to ferment.

INGREDIENTS

For the Cocktail

- 1 ounce Campari
- 1 ounce Mezcal
- 3/4 ounce sweet vermouth
- 1/4 ounce Simple Smoked Syrup

For the decoration

- 1 sliced orange on wheels

INSTRUCTIONS

1. Move the oven rack to high (about 3-4 inches from the flame) and preheat the broiler.

2. Dry the orange slices with a paper towel and place them on a 9x13 baking sheet. Place them in the grill and cook for 10 minutes on each side. Leave to cool.

3. Add ice to a glass with ice. Add Campari, mezcal, sweet vermouth and smoked simple syrup. Stir well and garnish with a charred orange wheel.

Smoked Manhattan

Another timeless cocktail with a sweet but robust flavour that can withstand smoke.

INGREDIENTS

- 2 parts rye
- 1 part sweet vermouth
- 2 dashes cocktail bitters

PREPARATION

1. Pour rye, sweet vermouth and bitters into a cocktail glass with ice. Stir.

2. Pour into a smoke-filled jar, shake for 30 seconds and leave for 2-5 minutes.

3. Pour into an Old Fashioned glass and garnish with a cherry.

Smoked Ash Blonde

A lighter concoction with a flavoured wine base. The floral and fruity sweetness creates an interesting canvas for a smoke infusion - just be careful not to overdo it. You only want to smoke for a few seconds.

INGREDIENTS

- 3 parts Lillet blanc
- 1 part Cointreau

- 1 splash sweet vermouth

PREPARATION

1. Pour the Lillet and Cointreau into a tin with ice, then shake.

2. Strain into a smoke-filled jar, shake for 30 seconds and pour into a coupe glass.

The Smoky Old Man

Inspired by a classic Old Fashioned cocktail and my 40-year-old brother who loves smoked food.

INGREDIENTS

- ½ teaspoon sugar can also be substituted with simple syrup
- 3 dashes Angostura bitters works well
- 2 oz Pendleton Midnight Whisky works great
- 1 large smoked ice cube
- 2 smoked cherries Maraschino cherries are an acceptable substitute

- 1 slice of orange peel about 2 inches long
- Dash of club soda optional

DIRECTIONS

1. In a cocktail shaker, add the sugar, bitters, whisky and some ice.
2. Shake well for about 10 seconds to dissolve the sugar.
3. Place the smoked ice cube in an old-fashioned glass and strain the drink into the glass.
4. Add 2 smoked cherries (or 1 maraschino cherry) and orange peel. Enjoy.

Rum & Smoke

On the surface, Rum & Smoke looks like little more than a hibernating Negroni rum. But stick it under a glass cloche with a sprig of flaming rosemary, and you have a sexy, smoky, cinematic cocktail.

INGREDIENTS

- 1 1/2 oz Aged Rum
- 3/4 oz Oloroso sherry

- 1/4 oz Tempus Fugit Gran Classico Bitter Liqueur
- 1 tablespoon Smoked Rosemary Simple Syrup*
- Garnish: Sprig of flamed rosemary

DIRECTIONS

1. In a mixing glass, add all ingredients over ice and stir until chilled.

2. Strain into a glass with fresh ice.

3. Garnish with a sprig of flamed rosemary.

4. Cover with a glass dome and leave for 1-2 minutes, or until the cocktail is well smoked, before drinking.

5. *Smoked rosemary simple syrup: In a saucepan over medium heat, combine 1/2 cup sugar, 1/2 cup water, and the zest of 1 orange and stir until just below a boil. Remove from heat. Using a kitchen torch or lighter, ignite a sprig of rosemary until it begins to smoke on all sides. Place the smoking sprig in a casserole dish and leave to infuse, covered, for 20 minutes. Strain out the solids and store in the fridge for up to a week.

Smoked Gin Tonic

An unusual twist on a classic gin and tonic, this drink uses slow-smoked ice cubes to add an extra layer of interest and flavour. With plenty of fresh, fruity lime to match the botanicals in the gin, the smoke harmonises beautifully with bitter notes of the tonic.

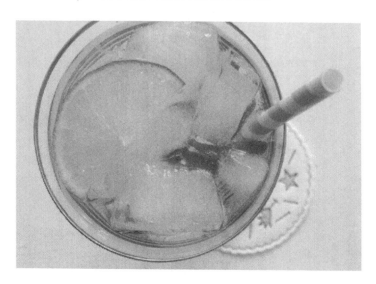

INGREDIENTS

- ice cubes, 10-15 smoked (see below)
- 1 lime, cut into 8 wedges
- 90ml gin, preferably citrusy (I used Brecon Botanicals)
- tonic water, preferably high quality (I used Fever Tree)

- 1 slice of lime, thin, cut in half (for garnish)

INDICATIONS

1. Squeeze the juice from two wedges per glass, then fill the glasses with the smoked ice cubes and the rest of the lime wedges

2. Add the gin and top up with the tonic. Garnish with half of the thin lime wedge and serve immediately

FRUITY

Pineapple Hibiscus Margarita

My invention is a fruity concoction that I created with my friends and colleagues. Organic Tequila Blanco is so smooth and delicate. It's the tequila you want to drink if you think you don't like tequila or you've had too many bad experiences with our college's crappy daily tequila.

Every time I open the bottle and take in the aroma, pineapple is always the first thing that comes to mind, so it's a no-brainer that I choose to make a pineapple margarita - I really had no other choice.

As Azuñia prides itself on being an organic tequila, I also like to keep my cocktails this way and only use organic ingredients in the drink. Ripe, buttery organic pineapple, organic lime from my tree and even organic granulated sugar in the syrup. It may sound a bit fussy, but I think it makes all the difference in the final drink.

The final touch is the hibiscus salt on the rim from The Spanish Tin. It has just a hint of smoky paprika smoke with all the tartness of the ground hibiscus flowers and the perfect amount of flaky sea salt. I highly recommend seeking it out, it has a seasoning for every occasion.

This Pineapple Hibiscus Margarita is made with fresh pineapple puree, organic blanco tequila and hibiscus syrup. Perfect for celebrating Cinco de Mayo!

FOR THE HIBISCUS SYRUP

- 2 cups water
- 2 cups caster sugar
- 1 cup of dried, rinsed hibiscus flowers

FOR THE MARGARITA

- Hibiscus salt or kosher salt
- 2 ounces of organic Tequila Blanco (Azuñia is my favourite)
- 2 ounces pineapple puree *see note
- 2 limes, juiced, plus more for garnish
- 1/2 ounce pineapple gum syrup
- 1/2 ounce hibiscus syrup
- pineapple wedges, for garnish

TO MAKE THE SYRUP:

1. Combine water, sugar and flowers in a small saucepan and place over medium heat. Whisk until sugar is dissolved and bring to a boil. Allow to simmer for 15 minutes.

2. Cover, remove from the heat and leave to cool. Strain and cool completely.

TO MAKE MARGARITA:

1. Rub a lime around the rim of a stone glass. Dip the outside of the rim in hibiscus salt to coat it. Fill the glass with ice.

2. Combine tequila, pineapple puree, lime juice and pineapple gum syrup with a scoop of ice in a cocktail shaker. Shake vigorously until combined and the outside of the shaker is filled with ice. Strain into the prepared glass. Pour over the

hibiscus syrup, garnish with a slice of lime and a slice of pineapple, if desired.

Smoking Blackberry Sage Margarita

I love making fun cocktails and this was definitely the most fun. How could it not be with smoked dry ice! It's going to take a bit of work to find some dry ice, but it was worth it. You know what's funny? Every person I talked to about dry ice felt the need to tell me that I shouldn't play with it and that it was dangerous. So I'm going to do my duty here and state the obvious....

DO NOT TOUCH DRY ICE, DO NOT EAT OR DRINK DRY ICE, DO NOT PASS GO WITH DRY ICE.

Seriously folks, dry ice is perfectly safe as long as you use tongs to handle it. It's also perfectly safe in cocktails, as long as you use food-grade dry ice and let it melt completely before enjoying your delicious concoction.

Okay, warning/warning over. Let's talk about this blackberry goodness. I'm a big fan of any berry, but blackberries and sage are a winning combination and I thought it would be perfect for Halloween. If you can't find dry ice or just don't want to use it, you can still make a "steaming" margarita by lighting a dried sage leaf just before serving. The aroma of sage burning only adds to the sage flavor profile in the drink. Plus it looks pretty spooky too!

INGREDIENTS

- 2 ounces 100% agave silver tequila
- 1 ounce lemon juice
- 8 medium blackberries
- 5 fresh sage leaves
- 1 teaspoon maple syrup
- 1 pinch of orange bitters

GARNISH (OPTIONAL)

- Dried sage leaves

- Blackberries
- Dry ice

INSTRUCTIONS

1. Stir the blackberries and sage together in a cocktail shaker until broken up and fragrant.

2. Pour in the tequila, lemon juice, bitters and maple syrup. Give it a good shake and pour over a cube of dry ice (if using) or regular ice if using the dried sage leaf. If using dried sage, light the tip on the fire just before serving.

The Smoking Gun

INGREDIENTS

- 1.33 oz Islay single malt whisky
- 0.67 oz Simple syrup
- 0.67 oz lemon juice
- 1,67 ounces of orange juice
- 0,83 oz Quail egg white
- 1,59 oz Passion fruit
- 0.04 oz Saffron
- 11.29oz Ice cubes

INDICATIONS

1. Fill a glass with ice to the top
2. Pour 0.7 oz of sugar syrup, 1.7 oz of orange juice and 0.7 oz of lemon juice into a shaker
3. Add 0.8 oz of quail egg whites and 1.3 oz of single malt Islay whisky
4. Shake gently without ice
5. Fill the shaker with ice cubes and shake once more
6. Strain into rocks glass
7. Garnish with saffron and half a passion fruit.

Orange Cranberry Smoked Cocktail

INGREDIENTS

● 11/2 cups cranberry juice

- 1/2 cup orange juice
- For Orange Cranberry Smoked Cocktail:
- 4-5 smoked ice cubes
- 2 oz vodka
- 3-4 oz orange juice
- 1 orange slice for garnish

INSTRUCTIONS

- In an aluminim pan or cast iron skillet pour in the cranberry juice and orange juice.
- Place pan into a preheated grill or smoker and close the lid.
- Smoke at 225 for about 45 minutes.
- Then carefully remove the pan and let liquid cool to room temperature.
- Pour liquid into ice cube tray and freeze.

For Orange Cranberry Smoked Cocktail

- In glass of choice, add the frozen smoked ice cubes.
- Add vodka, orange juice, and stir.
- Garnish with orange slice and serve.

The Boulevardier

INGREDIENTS

- 6 oz of bourbon (rye can also be used)
- 3 oz sweet vermouth
- 3 oz Campari
- Orange peel garnish

EQUIPMENT

- Cocktail Shaker
- Smoke gun, optional
- Glass decanter with stopper, optional

INSTRUCTIONS

1. Mix the bourbon, vermouth and Campari in a cocktail shaker with ice and stir until very cold. Strain into rocks glasses filled with ice. Add orange peel for garnish and serve immediately.

To add smoke:

2. Set up the smoking gun for each pack (fill with wood shavings - I recommend using cherry wood shavings, but apple or hickory also work well. The smoking gun listed here comes with the shavings included).
3. Pour bourbon, vermouth and Campari into a cocktail shaker with ice and shake until cold. Then pour into a container with a tightly fitting cork, ideally a glass decanter.
4. Insert the smoking gun tube into the mouth of the decanter. Ignite the pistol to fill the decanter with

wood smoke. Remove the hose, cap the decanter tightly and leave it sealed for 6-8 minutes. Then pour (drink and smoke) into cocktail classes with ice. Add orange peel for garnish and serve immediately.

The Fireside

Savour the aroma of winter with our grapefruit and maple syrup cocktail, enjoyed anywhere you like.

INGREDIENTS
- 100 ml Vodka
- 25 ml Organic maple syrup
- 1 a sprig Rosemary

- 1 pinch of salt
- 125 ml freshly squeezed pink grapefruit juice

DIRECTIONS
1. Prepare everything you need in advance to make the cocktail directly in front of your guests.
2. In the bottom of a low tumbler briefly crush the rosemary with maple syrup and salt.
3. Add quality ice and Vodka
4. Top with pink grapefruit juice and stir well.
5. Garnish with a sprig of rosemary.

Smoked Bloody Mary

Sure, this isn't an alcoholic drink, as we recommended above. But the salty brunch standby works great with a little smoke, especially if you garnish it with some crispy bacon.

INGREDIENTS

- 3 parts vodka
- 6 parts tomato juice
- 1 part lemon juice
- A dash of Worcestershire sauce
- Dash of Tobasco

- Salt
- Pepper

PREPARATION

1. Add the Worcestershire, Tobasco and a pinch of salt and pepper to a cocktail glass.
2. Pour in the vodka, tomato juice and lemon juice and mix thoroughly.
3. Pour into a smoke-filled jar, shake for 30 seconds and leave for 1-3 minutes.
4. Pour into a highball glass and garnish with celery, bacon and pickles.

Smoked Sazerac

Perfect for everyone, the Solstice Sazerac uses high-dry bourbon rather than rye whisky, which mutes the spicy flavours of the traditional Sazerac. "Cinnamon syrup adds a spicy baking element, and cinnamon smoke mixed with orange zest adds an interesting dimension to a well-known cocktail," explains Ben Potts, bar manager at Miami's Beaker & Gray.

INGREDIENTS

- 2 oz. Ransom High Rye Bourbon

- ¼ oz. cinnamon syrup (recipe below)
- 2 dashes Angostura Bitters
- 6 dashes Peychaud's Bitters
- Crushed cinnamon bark (for smoking)
- For garnish: orange peel, smoked cinnamon stick

DIRECTIONS

1. Chill a shot glass with ice, then discard the ice.
2. Combine the cocktail ingredients in a cocktail glass with ice.
3. Place crushed cinnamon bark on a plate or fireproof surface and light.
4. Cover with cold glass to catch the smoke. Stir cocktail in cocktail glass for five seconds. Remove the glass from the smoke, and slowly invert.
5. Strain the cocktail into a smoked glass very slowly.
6. Express the orange peel on top and serve with a smoked cinnamon stick on the side.

HOW TO MAKE THE CINNAMON SYRUP

- 1 cup sugar
- 1 cup water
- 3 crushed cinnamon sticks

Boil the sugar in water. Add the crushed cinnamon sticks and simmer for 10 minutes. Remove from the heat, leave to cool and strain into a glass bottle. Refrigerate for one month.

Dragon's Breath Cocktail

Here's a cocktail that smokes - literally - thanks to an upside-down brandy shot glass filled with mesquite smoke. It comes from a Moldovan bartender named Aleks Karavay whom I met in Scottsdale, Arizona. The Cointreau and St-Germain provide bittersweet notes of fruitiness. "Kill your inner beast," Karavay says. Amen.

INGREDIENTS

- 4 to 6 ice cubes (1 cup; for even more flavour, use smoked ice cubes)
- 2 ounces (4 tablespoons) bourbon (use your favourite)
- 1 teaspoon St-Germain
- 1 teaspoon Cointreau (or other orange liqueur)
- 1 teaspoon simple syrup or smoked simple syrup

INDICATIONS

1. Step 1: Load the smoker with sawdust and light it according to the manufacturer's instructions.

2. Step 2: Hold a shot glass of brandy upside down. Insert the tube of the smoker into the glass and fill it with smoke until you can see through the glass. Cover the glass tightly with a coaster to retain the smoke and turn it upright.

3. Step 3: Place the ice cubes in a shaker. Add the bourbon, St-Germain, Cointreau and simple syrup and stir quickly for about 20 seconds.

Step 4: Uncover the shot glass and strain the cocktail immediately. Serve immediately, with the smoke still dripping from the glass.

Smoked Rose Cocktail

Smoked rose is a fabulous scotch cocktail that brings a different smoky flavour to the mix. It's an aromatic delight and a brilliant new way to enjoy your favourite whisky.

This recipe comes from The Famous Grouse. It features one of the brand's signature blended scotch expressions, Smoky Black, which you may know better as The Black Grouse (it has recently been rebranded). The scotch provides a nice smoky, sweet background to this cocktail and it is highly recommended to stick to it.

The other 'smoke' in the cocktail comes from burning a sprig of dried rosemary to flavour the glass. Not only does it add flavour to the drink, but it fills the room with an inviting aroma that captures the attention of everyone present.

In support of this, rosemary syrup sweetens the cocktail and Green Chartreuse adds its seductive herbal matrix to the mix. Even if you don't smoke rosemary, it's a pleasant drink.

INGREDIENTS

- 1 cup water
- 1 cup sugar (white granules)
- 3 tablespoons of rosemary
- For the Cocktail
- 1 sprig of dried rosemary
- 2 ounces of Scotch whisky
- 1/4 ounce rosemary syrup
- 1/2 ounce Green Chartreuse

SYRUP INDICATIONS

1. Gather the ingredients.

2. In a small saucepan, bring the water to a slow boil.

3. Add the sugar and stir until completely dissolved.

4. Reduce the heat, add the rosemary and cover the saucepan. Leave to simmer for 15 minutes.

5. Remove the pan from the heat and allow the syrup to cool completely, keeping it covered.

6. Drain the rosemary and bottle the flavoured syrup in an airtight glass jar. It should be kept in the fridge and will keep for about 2 weeks.

COCKTAIL INDICATIONS

1. Smoke a coupe glass to flavour the inside: Light the sprig of dried rosemary on the fire, turn off the flame and place it inside the glass.

2. In a cocktail glass filled with ice, pour the Scotch, the rosemary syrup and the green Chartreuse. Stir well.

3. Strain into the smoked glass.

4. Serve and enjoy!

Smoky S'mores Root Beer Floats

A fun twist on a classic root beer float, using the flavours of S'mores and vanilla and chocolate ice cream. Plus the mix of chocolate and melted marshmallow goodness of S'mores!

INGREDIENTS

- 1/3 cup of melted milk chocolate chips
- 1 cup chocolate ice cream
- 1 cup vanilla ice cream
- 2 bottles of root beer
- pinch of smoked sea salt

- 2 tablespoons graham crackers
- 2 charred or burnt marshmallows

INSTRUCTIONS

1. To melt the chocolate chips, place them in a bowl and microwave in 30 second intervals until melted. I like to take a spoon and sprinkle this around the rim.
2. Fill each glass with chocolate and vanilla ice cream. Add a pinch of smoked sea salt to the glass. Pour in the root beer just before serving. Sprinkle graham crackers on top and add a charred marshmallow to finish. Devour!
3. As a note, you can char the marshmallows on a gas cooker, under the broiler (watch them all the time!) or even just melt them in the microwave if you don't have some sort of bonfire.

CONCLUSION

This book has come to the end. We have seen how the world of Mixology is in great ferment and never before has there been such a rich production of original and innovative cocktails. While at first glance the ingredients of a cocktail are always the same, the methods of execution and variations are many. The choice of ingredients, doses, glasses and glasses to be used are fundamental for the success of a good cocktail.

Behind the bar you can prepare drinks that date back to the dawn of bar culture and spirits, such as cocktails from the nineteenth and early twentieth centuries, contemporary cocktails, with both classic and innovative preparation techniques. The Barman Mixologist is often associated with bartenders with methodologies and service styles that bring back the vintage atmosphere of speakeasies, as was the custom in the years of Prohibition, when the bartender was an icon of transgression who allowed people to drink despite the prohibitions.

It is therefore very important, in addition to the recipe, to have the right tools to prepare and present the new cocktails in the best possible way because the customer is gratified with the eyes even before being gratified with the taste! Although not new in the world of mixology, the technique of smoking is gaining more and more ground and becoming a real trend.

Smoking can be either cold or hot: the former is carried out at temperatures ranging from 20°C to 45°C; the latter, on the other hand, is done at a temperature ranging from 50°C to 90°C. The methods for creating these 'steaming' cocktails are varied. They range from the use of pre-smoked spirits to the use of liquid smoke, but probably the method preferred by the masters of mixology is the use of the "choreographic" smoking-gun. The secret of the technique lies in its simplicity and above all in its versatility, which makes it possible to flavour any type of food, stimulating and satisfying the sensory and scenic properties of restaurant and bar customers. At the base of the process is the exposure of the food to the smoke generated by the combustion of wood or aromatic herbs, which, depending on their quality, give a characteristic flavour to all foods, including whisky, beer and various types of drink.

In the career of a bartender there always comes a time when you have to deal with all the techniques of mixing and processing products, raw materials and tools that we have at our disposal to work at our best and obtain better quality drinks.

What often happens, however, is that the enormous amount of equipment available on the market today and the ever-improving technology risk being proof of incapacity rather than enhancing the skills of a good bartender. Let me explain. Let's imagine that we have a latest generation watch with various functions, integrated messaging, call alerts, temperature indicator, altimeter, you name it. Oh yes, I forgot; every now and then it also tells you what time it is.

Now, how many of you know that, for example, in order for the temperature reading to be correct, it is best to remove the watch from your wrist for a few minutes so that the sensor detects the true ambient temperature and is not 'fooled' by the body temperature on your wrist? Or is it better to set the correct atmospheric pressure with reference to the standard atmospheric pressure of 1013 hpa, so that the instrument gives a real feedback?

With this example, I want you to realise that you don't need the latest technology to make great drinks, but you do need to know how to use the ones you have at your disposal well and rationally.

As I always say, remember that the best drinks in the world were made over a century ago, when technology, quality and hygiene of raw materials and products were certainly not what they are today. I hope you enjoyed this book, it's time to practice with your drinks!

Printed in Great Britain
by Amazon